Are the
Golden Years
Tarnished?

Are the Golden Years Tarnished?

Diane Manning

To order additional copies of this book, contact:
Xlibris Corporation
1-888-795-4274
www.Xlibris.com
Orders@Xlibris.com
88103

Contents

This book is lovingly dedicated to everyone who is young at heart, regardless of age.

I want to give special acknowledgement to:

Grace Calloway, a friend who has provided the incentive to continue writing despite many obstacles.

Ellis Regini for invaluable information on helping seniors cope with economic issues of retirement.

Teachers of my religious classes who have helped me with my search for a deeper understanding of G-d and my unique contribution to making this a better world.

Les Novitz, MD, who has restored my faith in the medical profession with his expertise as a diagnostician, his care and concern for his patients, and his respect for me as an individual.

Friends and neighbors who have shared their stories on many of the topics in this book.

Introduction

We have looked forward to our golden years from the time that the expression became popular. This was supposedly our reward for the dedicated years of hard work in our professions and as parents. Medical technology has given our generation the gift of living longer, high quality lives. We can retire and have financial security. Our children will leave the nest to build independent lives of their own. At last, we have the luxury of choosing what we want to do (singly or as a couple). We can revive old dreams, re-connect with long-lost friends, and explore the possibility of a new career. We are the luckiest generation.

Does this sound too good to be true? If it does, that is because it is! In today's economy, many of us have to continue to work just to pay the bills. Yes, we are living longer, with access to medical technology that can prevent and cure some illnesses. However, the longer we live, the more likely our bodies and minds will succumb to disease. We will also have to deal with loss as we grow older—of relatives and friends. As for the relief of responsibility from our independent children, I wonder how many of you still have adult children living at home, some with children of their own. In more and more families in today's society, grandparents are raising their grandchildren.

Have I succeeded in depressing you? I sincerely hope not. Otherwise, you won't read any further. I have interviewed many seniors, given programs on senior issues, and even written another book for seniors. What I have discovered is that we seniors are resilient, ethical, tenacious, and retain a positive attitude.

My purpose in writing this book is to explore the issues that seniors face in the 21st century, citing individual examples of how some have lived with adversity. I also want my readers to understand that, as a group, we still exert a powerful influence on future generations. They need our guidance, and we need to find a way to communicate this message to them. What we can teach them will be a valuable legacy.

I don't offer solutions. Most of all, I want you, the men and women of the senior generation, to be aware of your importance, and to make choices that will allow you to lead fulfilling lives into your eighties and nineties, while setting the example for those to come.

When you have finished this book, I hope that most of you will be able to answer the question in the title with a negative.

Chapter One

"ARE YOU READY FOR RETIREMENT?"

This is probably the most important chapter to read if you are planning retirement in the near future. As I write this chapter, the economic picture is bleak, and the stock market is volatile. Both of these factors impact decisions about retirement.

Seniors at age 65 have access to Medicare, which presently provides adequate medical coverage. However, the coverage is 80%, which means that you will require a supplement. You can go this route with basic Medicare or you can consider one of the many HMO packages offered. Necessary information can be acquired by calling 1-800-633-4227. The good news is, in my experience, there isn't a long wait to speak to someone, and the persons answering the phone are very helpful. If you have a computer, access *www.medicare.gov* for general information or *www.My*Medicare.gov. for individual information. I suggest that you request a copy of *Medicare & You* for the current year, which gives detailed information on everything covered. As for supplements, most people that I interviewed used AARP. All of the above sounds positive. There is, however, a major problem with Medicare. Many doctors are not accepting Medicare patients because the reimbursements have been cut, and it is not cost effective for them to continue to serve these patients. Your biggest problem will probably be finding qualified doctors who still accept Medicare patients. Be sure to research the issue. I also recommend that you explore the options of long term health care. The younger you are, the lower the cost. Medicare covers care after a medical procedure for a minimum amount of time. This insurance gives you the security of taking care of your needs indefinitely.

The next issue to consider is financial planning, including Social Security. Unlike Medicare, accessing Social Security is much more complicated. Married individuals can use their own Social Security or their spouse's, whichever is higher. Widows and widowers are eligible for a certain amount, as are those who are divorced, if they were married for at least ten years. However, if the ex re-marries before age 60 benefits are not payable until the subsequent marriage ends. There are additional rules for widows and widowers caring for a child, or for those who are disabled. It would be helpful to calculate the approximate amount of money that you (and your spouse) expect to receive. Don't forget that the age for maximum benefits has increased. It is still 65 for those who were born before 1938 but it rises gradually until it reaches 67 for those born in 1960 and later. The Senior Citizens' Freedom to Work Act eliminated the retirement earnings test for those who have attained full retirement age, but it still applies to beneficiaries. The phone number for Social Security is 1-800-772-1313. The Web site is *www.SocialSecurity.gov*. I received most of my information from a booklet entitled *Guide to Social Security*, which you can acquire by calling them or contacting them online.

The next step in financial planning for retirement includes pensions, investments, and any other sources of income that you have. I cannot stress enough the importance of consulting a reliable, credentialed financial planner to give you a total picture of your financial status. The main question to ask is, "Will you outlive your money?" In my case, I was forced to retire three years earlier than planned, and I didn't know the answer to that question. I consulted a financial planner who used the computer to calculate the years I would live, my income, lifestyle, and factored in inflation. The good news that I could retire just before my 60th birthday with financial security, was one of the best days of my life.

It was a tremendous sense of relief to know that I wasn't pressured to search for a job. I could sleep later than 4:30AM, and have the luxury of pursuing other interests. My current financial planner has invested my income according to my wishes—conservative, but allowing for inflation. I didn't truly appreciate his expertise until I discovered that I would have to pay substantial income tax on unearned income. At first, this was upsetting, until my accountant explained that paying taxes meant that my investments were earning money. It took awhile for me to adjust to this (I was still looking for a refund), but I am now totally comfortable with paying quarterly taxes.

Now that you have an overall view of your financial picture, you are ready to make the next necessary decisions that will affect your future. This is the most difficult part of the plan. Depending on your resources, you may have to continue to work, consider selling your home and living in smaller accommodations, and/or adjust your lifestyle. If you are fortunate, you will be able to retire with the peace of mind that you are financially stable for years to come.

There is one last piece of the picture that I want to discuss. This affects seniors with children and grandchildren. In an ideal situation, children assume responsibility for themselves at eighteen or when they graduate from college. Sometimes, however, that doesn't happen, and the depressed economy makes it even more difficult for this younger generation. Mothers, grandmothers, and great grandmothers come to the rescue, offering shelter, food, and encouragement. Short-term this can work, but long term there are problems, for both the older and the younger generations involved. For the retirees, it can be a drain on financial resources, impacting long-term plans for retirement. For those on the receiving end, they are denied the opportunity to assume responsibility for their own lives, with the sense of accomplishment that this brings. Definite rules should be made and agreed on by everyone. Those receiving the help should make every effort to get a job and begin contributing to the payment of rent, utilities, and food. Until they have a job, they should do necessary chores to maintain the household. Privacy should be respected by all parties. The goal should be for the child, grandchild or great grandchild to begin living independently as soon as possible, This would be a win-win situation for everyone concerned.

I will ask my readers at the end of each chapter to ask themselves the question that is the title of this book, "Are the Golden Years Tarnished?" The answer will not be the same for everyone, but please keep reading. You won't have the final answer until the last chapter.

Chapter Two

"HOW DO I FILL THE TIME?"

I have presented a program entitled "Transitions" to several senior groups since I have retired. This presentation is based on Gail Sheehy's book *New Passages*, an update of her first book on the same topic. She interviewed people in various stages of life. For seniors, mostly in their 50's and 60's, she asked, "How do you plan to spend your time in the retirement years?" Some of them responded that they could hardly wait to pursue activities such as traveling, volunteering, and spending more time with friends. Some, however, actually dreaded the day of retirement because they were afraid of being bored, and were at a loss as to how to fill the days.

From personal experience, I can assure you that retirement does not mean boredom. In fact, there are so many choices it might be difficult for some to make a decision. In this chapter, I have researched resources on popular activities with seniors that I interviewed. These include volunteering; traveling; continuing to work, either full-time or part-time; taking courses or even pursuing a degree; and taking a second look at an old unfulfilled dream. If you have good basic health, financial security, and a desire to live life to the fullest, anything is possible.

A popular choice for many retirees is volunteering. The Web site that I consulted gave an overview of possible volunteer activities for seniors, including organizations, programs, games, and other volunteer opportunities. Volunteers are welcome and needed in hospitals, nursing homes, shelters, schools, museums, and community events. It is important to choose a volunteer activity suited to your personality and background, and to decide how many days and/or hours you are willing to volunteer. The main benefit of volunteering is the reward that you receive for helping others.

Many retirees look forward to being able to travel, both inside and outside of the U.S. The economy has impacted travel plans for everyone, including seniors, but there are still ways to achieve this goal. Travel discounts are given to seniors by AAA, AARP, national parks, and some airlines. If you have a computer, check out the Seniors Discount Site. Elderhostel is a non-profit organization that coordinates almost 8,000 trips a year. These trips include room and board, activities, and primary transportation. Seniors can choose group trips, one-of-a-kind adventures, learning programs, or volunteer vacation excursions. There are other sites that can be helpful. I will give the Web sites at the end of the book.

For those who need (or want) to continue working, there are many resources that can provide information on both fulltime and part-time employment for seniors. AARP is one of the best resources. This Web site gives information on phased retirement, starting your own business, job hunting tips, employee rights and benefits, and work life. Another site lists specific jobs to consider, including the top 30, different options to consider, and market strategies, with additional resources. Some of the options include turning a hobby into a business or offering your services as a consultant. Another site categorizes jobs that maximize thinking skills and those that require physical skills. Needless to say, for those who need or want to continue working, there are many resources for those who are willing to dedicate the time to explore them.

Some seniors decide to fulfill an education goal. This can range from completing high school graduation requirements to taking post-graduate courses which may or may not include obtaining a degree. There is help on the Internet for this also. Many Web sites match degrees to specific universities with instructions on how to apply. The majority of the courses are offered online. One site gives information on how to find education resources in your local community. Another offers an article entitled "How to Get Free Education as a Senior Citizen". You can become a computer tech, chef, teacher, or lawyer. You are limited only by your abilities, interests, and motivation.

By now, I hope that everyone reading this chapter will agree that retirement does not mean the end of a fulfilling life. In fact, depending on your choices, this can be a "golden" time.

I saved the best for last. We all have dreams as children for what we want to be as adults, most of which are forgotten as we deal with the realities of everyday life. I dreamed of becoming a blues singer because I had some talent in music. I also wanted to be able to play the piano the way my very talented mother did. I ignored the fact that she took lessons for years, and spent five hours a day practicing. In fact, when she took me to her piano teacher for lessons, I quit after a few months because I didn't want to practice. In later years, I regretted this decision because I realized, even if I wasn't a concert pianist, I could have played and sung for my own personal enjoyment. I compromised after retirement by taking a few basic classes that allowed me to play using chords. I discovered that I could actually play certain simple songs, such as nursery rhymes. There was a sense of satisfaction in achieving this, and an added benefit in giving my arms and fingers much-needed exercise.

Take a second look at those childhood dreams. Maybe you won't become a research scientist, astronaut, or celebrity, but it might be possible to develop a talent that has been on the back burner for most of your adult life. You might be surprised at what you will discover.

As promised, I am again asking the question, "Are the golden years tarnished?" This chapter should give some hope that they are not, with all of the possibilities available for living a full life.

Chapter Three

"SURVIVING THE ODDS"

The good news is—we are living longer. The bad news is—we are living longer. Let me explain this seeming contradiction.

Experts tell us that we are indeed living longer. In fact, the number of centenarians is increasing, and many of us today will live to be eighty or ninety. Modern technology is a major factor in prolonging life. It has provided cures and treatments for many diseases. In some cases, however, the technology has extended the years but not the quality of life, which gives families of this generation problems that their parents and grandparents didn't have.

How can we deal with this, or is it just a foregone conclusion over which we have no control? In my first book, one of the chapters was entitled "You Can't Escape

Your Roots". In this chapter, I discussed family history, but also the importance of knowing who you are—physically, mentally, and emotionally. Research for my book led me to an Internet article by the Association for psychological Science entitled "Nature, Nurture, Nuance". This article reported that molecular-genetic technology has made the either/or argument less important with the focus now on the interplay between heredity and environment. Genetic history does impact your health and well being, but lifestyle can make a difference too. So if we know that a close relative died of a stroke or heart disease or cancer, we can pay particular attention to prevention in those areas before they become major problems.

You may want to skip this part of the chapter. I have to include this information, even though everyone has been bombarded through the media with its importance. Lifestyle makes a difference! General guidelines include the following. 1) Eat a balanced diet, 2) Exercise, 3) Learn to manage stress, 4) Get enough sleep, 5) Drink lots of water, 6) Schedule regular medical exams, 7) Stay socially active, 8) Don't smoke, 9) Drink alcohol in moderation, 10) Maintain a positive attitude towards life.

I want to emphasize the importance of exercising your brain as well as your body. As we grow older, we are at increased risk for some type of dementia (stroke, Alzheimer's, etc.) which can be just as devastating as cancer or heart disease. Aging does not automatically mean loss of mental ability. One article I researched listed three myths about aging. Myth: Old age means poor health and disability. Fact: There are some diseases that are more common in older adults. However, getting older does not mean poor health or that you will be confined to a wheelchair. Refer to the preventive strategies in the previous paragraph. Myth: Memory loss is an inevitable part of aging. Fact: You may eventually notice that you don't remember experiences as easily as in the past, and memories may take longer to retrieve. However, significant memory loss is not an inevitable result of aging. Myth: You can't teach an old dog new tricks. Fact: One of the more damaging myths of aging is that after a certain age, you just won't be able to try anything new or have anything worthwhile to contribute. Quite the contrary is true. Older adults are just as capable of learning new things, thriving in new environments, and sharing wisdom and experience with many generations.

Keeping the above in mind, I offer resources on staying mentally alert, which include improving your memory, brain games, and cross training your brain. I will mention a few, and let you use my resources listed at the end of the book to provide other strategies.

One Web site gave general guidelines to improve memory. These include the following. 1) Don't get distracted. 2) Tailor information acquisition to your learning style (visual, auditory, etc.). 3) Involve as many senses as possible to tasks. 4) Relate information to what you already know. 5) Organize information. 6) Understand and be able to interpret complex material. 7) Rehearse information frequently. 8) Be motivated and keep a positive attitude. Another Web site listed five types of brain games to keep your mind fit. These activities included crossword puzzles, sudaku, brain puzzles, brain teasers, and brain training. A computer is very helpful in accessing this information, but your local bookstore can provide puzzles and brain teasers. One Web site, Masters of Healthcare, gives five pages of games and activities to challenge your mind.

There is a wonderful Web site, About.com, that allows individuals to share stories on aging. This provides a two-way benefit. You are able to read stories of people who have survived into their 80's, 90's, and even 100's, as told by younger relatives. You also have the opportunity of sharing your own story. I read a few of these stories, which were both encouraging and inspirational. There were a variety of reasons given for the longevity. Some relatives considered it "just plain luck", since the people described didn't live a healthy lifestyle. Some even smoked and ate an unhealthy diet most of their lives. For the majority, however, various reasons were given. These included staying active, having a positive attitude, adhering to a healthy diet, exercise, plenty of sleep, and embracing spirituality. One woman was a special inspiration. At the age of 70 she became a watercolor and Chinese calligraphy artist. At 75, she traveled alone to India, sleeping on trains. At 80, she learned how to snorkel in Cuba. I would never have attempted these activities in my 20's.

The news gives us examples also of special seniors. George Bush senior bailed out of an airplane on his 80th birthday. Our Supreme Court justices and many other politicians continue to serve their country into their 80's and 90's. Grandma Moses remains a shining example of someone who began an art career in later years.

My first book, which was dedicated to seniors, especially those with whom I had a personal connection, served as an inspiration on this topic. The paternal side of my family included strong women, several of whom survived into their 90's. Genetics played a part, but, taking a second look at their history, I discovered a toughness of character, a resilience that helped me to survive my personal losses. My Aunt Frieda died at the age of 98. She possessed the qualities of the resilient women from my dad's side of the family. I loved visiting her, never tiring of hearing her stories of growing up in Houston, and surviving the loss of her husband when she was in her 30's. She raised three young children with a minimum of resources. She managed to purchase a house, and provide all of her children with a college education. Infirmity took its toll, but until the end, she remained independent, refusing to leave her house and precious plants, and reading even though she suffered with macular degeneration. I miss our special talks.

I could recount more examples, but I am sure that you get the idea. I hope that you are thinking of your own personal stories.

This chapter is about surviving the odds. I hope, after reading it, you will agree that we don't have to accept genetic determination for our fate. We can beat the odds, and live longer, healthier lives.

Once again, I ask the question. "Are our golden years tarnished?" This chapter should give seniors hope that these years can be extended and remain golden.

Chapter Four

"LOSS"

Any book devoted to senior issues has to discuss this topic. Loss occurs throughout our lives, but it becomes a more vital issue as we grow older. My focus in this chapter is on the loss of loved ones, loss of physical and mental abilities, and, perhaps most important of all, loss of independence. I promise to end this chapter on a positive note as we once again ask the question, "Are our golden years tarnished"?

If you can locate this book, please read *Necessary Losses* by Judith Viorst. She is a well-known author who has outlined the losses that we experience in life with much research and intuition. Part four, chapters 16 - 20, "Loving, Leaving, Losing, Letting Go", discusses senior issues. I want to quote a paragraph in the introduction to the book, which defines loss. "When we think of loss we think of the loss, through death, but also by leaving and being left, by changing and letting go and moving on. And our losses include not only our separations and departures from those we love, but our conscious and unconscious losses of romantic dreams, impossible expectations, illusions of freedom and power, illusions of safety, and the loss of our younger self, the self that thought it would always be unwrinkled and invulnerable and immortal."

A few years ago, I presented a workshop on loss at a local senior care facility. In the second session, I discussed loss of loved ones, other losses, and a look to the future. I talked to my audience about the loss of a parent, a spouse, a child, grandchild, a sibling, other relatives, and friends. I also talked to them about loss through divorce, which can be as devastating (or more so) as loss through death. Another loss that I experienced was that a daughter married and subsequently moved to another state. She moved twelve years ago, and I still feel the loss of the opportunity to spend time with her and to have a relationship with my grandchildren. Likewise, friends may move away and we lose contact with them over the years.

I then discussed the stages of mourning, which include denial of loss, disorganized behavior, and adaptation. I emphasized that each individual needs to mourn in his or her own way, in his own time. I also gave coping techniques, which included cherishing memories, religious ceremony and rituals, support from family and friends, staying busy, focusing on others, support groups, and, if necessary, individual counseling. I attended a bereavement group for six months after the death of my husband. This helped because I was able to share my grief experiences with others and even made new friends. Rituals can also be helpful. Funerals, wakes, social gatherings of friends and neighbors who attend services and bring food to the bereaved offer support. In the Jewish religion, the widow (or widower) attends services morning and evening everyday until the unveiling of the tombstone, which occurs eleven months from the date of death. This ceremony marks the official end of mourning. During this year, the survivor has an opportunity to discover new strengths that will enable him/her to deal with the future.

In session three I talked about the physical and mental losses of aging. I also discussed financial loss (especially for women), and the loss of independence that occurs when seniors are no longer able to take care of themselves. This situation is often triggered by the necessity of giving up your beloved car, and many seniors fight this loss until they have no choice. All of the above losses affect our self esteem, which is crucial to survival. Fortunately, there are resources available to help seniors cope. There are many volunteer agencies, including AARP, that offer support. This support can range from providing the necessities, such as meals on wheels, to social support through groups and activities. Computers provide seniors with any number of resources (as I have discussed in previous chapters). They can also be an avenue of communication with others through email, and there are Web sites for playing games of all kinds.

In the fourth and final session, I talked about the future. I referred to authors such as Judith Viorst, Tom Monte, who wrote *Staying Young*, and Hugh Downs, author of *Taking charge*. These authors agreed on basic reasons for the ability of some seniors to cope with loss and to lead active lives. In general, seniors were advised to take good care of themselves, physically and mentally; to stay optimistic; to reduce stress in their lives; to commit to activities and goals; and to access their own creativity. The session ended on a positive note.

I began this chapter with a quote from Judith Viorst, author of *Necessary Losses*. Because I believe that her book has so much to offer seniors, I am including more detailed information. The last part of the book is entitled Loving, Losing, Leaving, and Letting Go. The first chapter discusses love and mourning. In this chapter the author gives specific information on the stages of mourning. After the initial shock and disbelief has worn off, survivors of loss move to a longer phase of intense psychic pain, which can include weeping and lamentation, emotional swings and physical complaints, lethargy, hyper-activity, regression to a needier stage, separation anxiety, despair, and anger. The anger can be directed towards the deceased person for abandoning us. Guilt is another strong emotion. We experience guilt for negative acts on our part in the relationship. We compensate for this by idealizing the one who died as "perfect". We may also attempt to summon them up through fantasies and dreams. This "summoning up" is an important step. In this way, we feel that we can manage to persuade ourselves that the person we lost is still here. I have to add my own observations on this stage through personal experience and research. Sometimes the guilt is simply based on the fact that we are alive and they are not. An attempt at reparation can also be re-inventing ourselves to be like the deceased person, another way of keeping them alive. I resolved to be more like my husband, who was unselfish, giving, and patient, not traits that I possessed. The final stage that the author cites is the completion of mourning or adaptation to our loss. The time frame may be different for each individual, but we eventually reach this stage in the grieving process. It will include some degree of recovery, acceptance, and adaptation. Life must go on.

Chapter two, "Shifting Images", gives the reader a glimpse of the heart and soul of loss. The author discusses the effects of loss on our definition of who we are. If we see ourselves through the eyes of others, we come to the realization that this image changes over time. We have to let go of some youthful dreams. We may never become neurosurgeons or astronauts, and won't be able to save the world. As the losses increase, we become more aware of our mortality. We question once sacred values, and our purpose in life. Integration will not occur without our ability to let go of these impossible dreams so that we can move forward. In this way, we discover a new self, one with the experience of the past, more confident in our ability to meet the challenges of the future.

Chapter three, "I Grow Old", confronts the reader with the realities of aging. Still, the basic message is positive. The senior years are sub-divided into three stages: the young-old (65 to 75), the middle old (75 to 85), and the old old (85 plus). This categorization of age lightened my spirit. I could feel younger than the next two groups, and look at them to see what would come next. The author gives tips for aging well, based on her interviews with seniors of all ages. She advises that it is easier to grow old if we are "neither bored or boring, if we have people and projects that we care about, if we are open and flexible and mature enough to submit to immutable losses." It is also possible for us to connect to the future through people, ideas, and the leaving of a personal legacy.

Chapter nineteen is entitled "The ABC of Dying". Most people want to avoid this topic, even in old age. I decided that confronting it would help me to deal with the fear of dying. There are many examples of people of all ages who have faced death bravely, concentrating on what they can accomplish while they are alive. They held every moment as precious gifts, to be used in accomplishing certain goals. Religion is another way in which people prepare for their exit from this life. Over the past ten years, I have taken religious courses that have given me valuable information in my search for a belief in the afterlife. I have also read books and articles on this topic. I have yet to experience a defining moment, such as a dream or vision from my husband or parents. Still, I am closer to a belief in the existence of an afterlife, and thus am less afraid of death. The author supports the journey of each person to search for belief, connection, and meaning in life as preparation for the next one, acknowledging that we may choose different ways to achieve this.

Researching the topic of loss on the Internet provided Web sites with information and resources. AARP, always a reliable resource, discusses some of the basic questions for widows and widowers concerning loss, through articles and interviews. This site also gives a list of services available, including support groups, publications, and community resources. The Help Guide gives both general and specific information about different types of loss, including symptoms, stages, and suggestions for coping. About.com provides more specific information on dealing with the death of a spouse. Some of these are especially helpful, given the confused mental and emotional state of the survivor. I will name a few of these suggestions. 1) Ask the funeral home for 6 to 8 copies of the death certificate. 2) Keep social security, bank accounts, and insurance information handy. 3) Set up a file for copies of everything that has to do with the estate. 4) Change bank accounts and file insurance claims. 5) Notify Social Security, organizations, banks, auto registration, credit card companies, and financial planners of the death of your spouse. 6) Don't pay any bills you are unsure of until you verify their authenticity. 7) Stay in charge of your own life. 8) Avoid hasty decisions. My attorney helped me with these tasks, but a written guide would have been very much appreciated.

A few sites gave tips for getting through the holidays, especially the first year. *Bereavement Magazine* was the best resource. The article advised mourners to express their feelings, as for what they needed from others, resolve how to spend the holidays. Try something new and different, or even substitute another activity if observance is still too painful. After my mother died, my aunt (who had lost her husband) and I decided to hold our annual Passover Seder at her daughter's apartment. It was smaller, but the change of place allowed us to deal with this holiday emotionally in a better way.

Learnwell.org provides a three hour online continuing education course on "Aging Well: Combating the Changes of Aging". This course is an overview of physical and mental changes that occur in aging, with specific suggestions for adapting and coping.

In the beginning of this chapter, I stated that loss of independence was especially devastating for seniors. Losing the ability to drive can have a major impact on lifestyle and emotional well being. If you are fortunate enough to afford a personal chauffer, it is possible to cope with this loss. I am reminded of one of my favorite films, "Driving Miss Daisy". Most people, however, cannot afford this luxury. There are other solutions. Start with your community. Consider public transportation, paying a small fee to neighbors and friends, and contacting organizations such as AARP for other options.

It is possible to write an entire book on this topic, but my purpose was to cover the basics, emphasizing that there are many ways to not only cope but to grow as a person through the experience of loss. Judith Viorst, in the last chapter of her book, "Reconstruction", expresses her thoughts and feelings on this topic. She says, "As for our losses and gains, we have seen how often they are inextricably mixed. There is plenty we have to give up in order to grow. We cannot deeply love anything without becoming vulnerable to loss. And we cannot become separate people, responsible people, connected people, reflective people without some experience of losing and leaving and letting go."

Once more, readers, thinking about loss, I ask you to answer the question, "Are our golden years tarnished?" For me, there are bright spots and much hope in the years ahead. I hope that you will agree.

Chapter Five

"DO YOU MISS THE GOOD OLD DAYS?"

Do you miss the serenity of silence in a world without computers, cell phones, answering machines, and television? Do you yearn for a world where families shared conversation at dinnertime, parents made the rules (which children followed without argument), and children could play outside after dark in relative safety? How many of you can remember driving from one location to another without using a freeway or encountering ongoing construction? Did we always dread predicted rainfall because our streets and/or homes might flood?

These were some of the questions that I asked in a presentation of this topic to a senior citizens group a few years ago. The audience shared my conflicted feelings about our quality of life today, and whether technology was a blessing or a curse. We explored these (and other issues) together, recalling positive memories of the "good old days"—the 30's, 40's and 50's—versus the complexity and dangers of the 21ˢᵗ century.

It wasn't difficult to make a case for having a better quality of life in many ways even 20 years ago. Life was definitely simpler without the noise and necessary maintenance of today's technological devices. We felt safer—both from natural disasters and from perpetrators of crime. Families usually gathered together for the dinner hour and engaged in conversation. In today's world, given parents' work schedules and extra-curricular activities for children, families rarely share a dinner hour. Forget meaningful conversation. There is constant interruption from cell phones, answering machines, Ipods, television, etc. Parents struggle to set rules for their children but have trouble enforcing them. They are influenced (and sometimes intimidated) by society, the media, and experts on child rearing in their desire to be good parents. The results often lead to a child-centered home without necessary guidelines and boundaries. In schools, the rules keep changing. Many children today (if they graduate) are not learning to read, write, or perform basic math skills. Add to these problems the constant reminder from an ever-present media that we are on the brink of environmental disaster, a possible World War III, and the imminent threat of Armageddon.

It would seem logical for those of us who remember simpler times to want to return to that life. Since that isn't possible, my audience and I found advantages to life in the 21st century. No one was anxious to live in a world without air conditioning, with refrigerators that needed to be defrosted, having to wash clothes by hand and hanging them out to dry, and, yes, television. We also couldn't ignore the medical technology that is making it possible for our generation to live longer and better lives. Some of us agreed that we could adapt to the use of computers, digital cameras, and cell phones (with the proper instruction). Maybe we can help our children and grandchildren to appreciate their heritage, and to slow down the pace of life enough to appreciate and enjoy each other.

The bottom line is that we can preserve what was valuable from the "good old days" while learning how to adapt to the technology and realities of today's world. Working in partnership with the younger generation might make all the difference for future generations.

This issue not only doesn't tarnish our golden years, it provides a sense of hope for a better future.

Chapter Six

"COMMUNICATION—A LOST ART"

Not too many years ago, the telephone was the only way to "reach out and touch someone"—relatives, friends, doctors, service persons, etc. Without an answering machine to run interference, it was necessary to answer the phone in order not to miss a call. The answering machine solved this problem by giving us the ability to screen our calls. We can avoid talking to vendors, surveyors, and people we know but wish to avoid. Unfortunately, this works both ways. Making an appointment for a routine physical examination or to obtain service for a household appliance can involve time, patience, and the ability to press the right buttons. A particular frustration to me is, after succeeding in scheduling an appointment to service an appliance, I am told that someone must be available from 9:00AM to 5:00PM to answer the door. Also, if the repairperson calls and no one answers the phone, they will go to the next appointment. I have on occasion been rude to the person giving me this news. Since I live alone, does this mean that I will be unable to use the restroom or take a shower for fear of missing this phone call? Usually, with persistence, I am able to negotiate a compromise, but why should I have to? I am the customer.

The use of email has taken us a step further in having the ability to communicate minus the frustration of using the phone and/or answering machine. In fact, I often prefer the use of email because I can choose when to reply to a message, and have time to think about what to say. This is especially helpful in communicating with relatives. If you are angry with your spouse for not remembering your birthday or with a friend who failed to return a borrowed item, the tone of your voice will most likely be affected in a verbal exchange. This could then lead to a reaction from the other person, causing more hurt feelings. With email, you can write, edit, and then send your message. This tool has probably been responsible for salvaging many relationships.

Cell phones and text messaging have provided instant communication for those of us who are impatient with the phone and email. I haven't learned to use either of these devices, and probably won't. I have a cell phone reserved for emergencies, but prefer to keep my phone conversations private. Nor do I wish to listen to other people's conversations in the grocery store or the doctor's office. I can't imagine having a use for text messaging, although I would be willing to learn in order to have a closer relationship with my grandchildren.

Sometimes it is not possible to avoid face-to-face communication. My years of teaching and counseling have provided some strategies that can help. Again, let me stress that this is information that you can choose to use or to ignore. I often told students in counseling sessions to "listen with your eyes, your ears and your brain". The message was to look at the person speaking, hear what they were saying, and process the meaning of what they were saying. Listening to the other person in this way is the first step in positive communication. If someone "pushes your buttons", it is O.K. to express your feelings about this, but use "I" statements. When your spouse says, "We are depositing money in the bank, not spending it on your ridiculous idea of a Hawaiian vacation", take a deep breath and respond, "I feel very hurt that when we disagree you call my ideas ridiculous". This will get better results than saying, "What about your ridiculous idea last summer of buying a boat?" The third suggestion is to pay attention to body language. You would be amazed at what this can reveal. Be aware of posture, facial expression, and arm and hand position. With teenagers, rolling their eyes is still a popular way to let you know they are tuning you out.

Let's face it. In today's world, communication has become a lost art. Maybe we can hide behind our technology in order to avoid communicating with others. This may be a temporary solution, but what effect does it have on relationships?

How can our generation use our knowledge and experience to improve communication for ourselves and for future generations? The answer to this question will help us to answer the question that I ask in every chapter. What do you think? "Are our golden years tarnished, or can we make them better?"

Chapter Seven

"FAMILIES AND RELATIONSHIPS—WHAT'S NORMAL?"

I could easily write a book on this topic. In the broadest sense, it covers everything from close family relationships to relationships with the post person, the grocery store clerk, and your Internet service provider. For the sake of brevity, I will focus on close family relationships—and, most important of all, the relationship that you have with yourself. First, it is necessary to have an understanding of the family unit.

The Bible (both the old and the new testaments) describes Adam and Eve as the first family. Everyone is familiar with this story. When they disobeyed God and ate the fruit of the Tree of Knowledge of Good and

Evil, they were cast out of Eden. Adam was sentenced to work for a living, and Eve would bear children with pain. I suspect that if Adam and Eve had a clue as to what was in store for them, they would have refrained from eating the fruit. They became the parents of Cain and Abel, whose sibling rivalry led to the first murder. Are we getting a clue yet? This first family was definitely dysfunctional by any standard, setting a pattern for future generations.

Originally, the word "family" meant a band of slaves. This definition endured for many centuries, even after the word came to apply to people affiliated by blood and marriage. Today, the concept of family includes many new definitions. In addition to the traditional nuclear family consisting of adult parents and their children, there are single parent families, those with parents who choose not to marry, and those with non-traditional partners such as gay and lesbian couples. Regardless of how a family is defined, researchers and psychologists agree that it must provide stability, support, structure, and values for all family members. Dr. Phil McGraw outlines the factors for creating a phenomenal family and the tools to accomplish this in his book *Family First*. No family is perfect. Most of us, if we were lucky, had parents who loved us, and did the best job of parenting possible with the knowledge available for their generation. Regardless of our family background, as adults we become responsible for taking charge of our lives. That includes how we relate to others.

A Web site that I consulted on this topic included an article that stated, "The quality of our partnerships with others actually reflects the quality of the relationship that we have with ourselves". This article was discussing the search for a significant other, but it could apply to most relationships. Think about it. The way we feel about ourselves is a major factor controlling the choices we make that attract others to us, and he quality of our relationships. If everyone knew this secret, we might not be coping with a 50% divorce rate in this country. We also might be able to have more positive relationships with our parents, siblings, children, coworkers, and friends. Since there is no way to escape from ourselves (although many spend a lifetime trying), we can instead spend this time and energy getting to know ourselves and trying to change what we don't like. If we are able to accept ourselves (strengths and weaknesses) without judgment, it would be easier to accept others. Rabbi Harold Kushner's book *How Good Do We Have To Be?* is a good resource for this idea. His book offers an insightful explanation of how, in our relationships with God and with others, we are not expected to be perfect. He explains that, if we understand this, our hearts and minds can be open to the acceptance of others, and we can lead more fulfilling lives. I am not saying that this is easy. If you aren't yet discouraged, please continue.

Our relationship with each of our parents is the first that we experience. One Web site listed basic rules in these relationships that will affect all others that we experience. The first rule is: "Anything unresolved with parents will come up in the person's other relationships." The second is: "Since established our first relationship with our parents, we tend to re-create their personality type as closely as possible in our other relationships." The third is "We tend to re-create the kind of relationship we had with our parents to other relationships." The fourth is "We will tend to copy the relationship our parents had with each other." This sounds like a set-up. Are we then destined to follow a certain pattern? Not necessarily. If we understand this concept (and ourselves), we can make a conscious effort to change the pattern. This means forgiving our dad for his disapproval, our mother for not always providing unconditional love, and both of our parents for not being perfect. We can begin to meet these needs for ourselves, which leads to maturity, and the ability to have positive relationships with others. It is also important to understand that this is a lifelong relationship that evolves. To make it work, it is necessary to accept the inevitable changes that occur. One day our roles will be reversed. Our parents will need us in the same way that we needed them as children. How much easier this is if we have established a relationship based on honesty, respect, trust, and love.

If you grew up with brothers and/or sisters, you endured the joys (and horrors) of this experience. On the plus side, there was always a playmate available. You were able to learn (through sibling rivalry) how to share toys as well as the attention and love of your parents. There is a downside. None of us really wants to share—either our toys, or, especially, the attention and love of our parents. We also want to have our own friends, space, and identity apart from our pesky brother or sister. Most of us outgrow the childhood years, and become friends as adults. Some, though, harbor grudges that carry over into our lives as adults that we may never resolve. Like the relationship with our parents, that with our siblings should be nurtured and cherished. Why? Because siblings share a common history that is unique. When our parents are gone, these shared memories can provide comfort and help to sustain the loss. Siblings can also be the ones to provide support during difficult times. Yes, you have to put effort into the relationship, and that means not only accepting the imperfections of your brothers and sisters but of their families as well. My brother and I re-established a relationship when circumstances brought him back to Houston after 28 years. I was a widow, and felt grateful to have a close relative in my life. The relationship requires constant work. Our priorities, personalities, and lifestyles are different. We could never live together, but we can continue to share happy and unhappy occasions, making them more meaningful.

We have survived the early years, come to terms with our relationships with our parents, our siblings, and ourselves, and now stand on the threshold of maturity. We are ready to embrace a career—and, perhaps, to search for a life partner. We could learn much from the matchmakers of past generations who matched couples based on their backgrounds and other qualities of compatibility. Often, the bride and groom didn't meet until the day of the wedding. These marriages not only survived, they thrived. If it were possible to combine the "chemistry" with basic values, background, character, etc., we would have the foundation for a good match. Ironically, today's young people with their busy lives are turning to Web sites such as Jdot.com for help. If they are reputable, the people who run these sites do the screening, leaving the client to choose from a variety of possibilities. These sites weren't available when I was searching for a life partner, so I went to singles parties, and even trusted blind dates. I always felt that I was fortunate to have found someone who was my "B'shert" (chosen mate), but, thinking back, maybe more than luck was involved. For one thing, the timing was right. I had reached an age (25) when my desire for motherhood influenced my selectivity, and hastened my search for

"Mr. Right". My husband was also ready to make his search for a mate more serious. Still, we dated for two years before making the final decision. Our marriage wasn't perfect (none is), but it was "as good as it gets". I attribute this to love, commitment, maturity, similar values, and a solid sense of humor.

Most couples want to be parents. This completes the cycle of our lives. We begin with ourselves; establish relationships with our parents, siblings, friends, and search for a life partner. Then, together, we begin the cycle again, vowing to be "perfect" parents. If we are fortunate enough to be blessed with healthy, "normal" children, we soon discover that, not only can we not expect to be "perfect" parents, this is truly the hardest job that we will ever have (and the most rewarding). At this point, I could refer my readers to another book I wrote based on my column "Creative Parenting". I will share the heart and soul of my philosophy on parenting.

Based on my years of experience as a teacher, counselor, mother, and grandmother, I have developed what I call the "Ten Principles of Parenting".

1.   Parents need to realize that their lifestyle has to change.
2.   It is important that both parents agree on parenting issues—at least, in the presence of their children.

3. Parents should be consistent in all aspects of parenting.
4. You will not be "perfect" parents—no one is—but you can be "good enough" parents.
5. Children are resilient. Even if their parents make mistakes (and they will), they will survive and be O.K.
6. You are the expert on your child. If you doubt the advice of professionals, get another opinion.
7. Take care of yourself.
8. Make your relationship with each other a priority.
9. The most important gift that you give to your children (besides unconditional love) is a set of principles and values.
10. Your most important role as a parent is to raise your child to have positive values, to be independent, and then to let go—in stages, according to their age.

Now you are ready to attend family reunions class reunions, and to survive encounters with people who may test your positive attitude. If nothing else works, try to remember that you won't have to see them again until the next family gathering.

I have included this chapter in a book on retirement because I believe that the maintenance of positive relationships is a lifelong process that becomes more important as we grow older. Positive relationships with family and friends can, hopefully, allow us to have a negative answer to the question "Are our golden years tarnished?"

Chapter Eight

"WHATEVER HAPPENED TO GOOD MANNERS?"

I rarely eat at restaurants or go to the movies anymore. These are activities that I used to enjoy, but find to be more relaxing in the comfort and tranquility of my home. Many people of all ages also dine at home and rent or tape movies for convenience. I have another reason as well. Venturing into the outside world to socialize is becoming too stressful to be worth the effort. Let me give you a few examples.

One of the last times that I remember eating at a restaurant, my friends and I had the misfortune to be seated close to a couple with young children. No one expects "perfect" manners from young children, but these two were allowed to run free in the restaurant, yell and scream, and throw food. Needless to say, this behavior was not conducive to a pleasant, relaxed atmosphere for dining. The parents made no effort to control their children's behavior.

It has been even longer since I went to a movie theater. After coping with conversation during the movie, obstruction of the screen by people who chose not to care whether they were blocking someone's view, and a need to use the restroom facilities during a critical part of the movie, I decided that using my VCR (or DVD) to rent or tape movies was a better option. Simple shopping excursions expose us to clerks who act as though they are doing the customer a favor to check our merchandise, and forget about asking for help to locate items (some clerks are incredibly nice and helpful). Road rage, an extreme example of rudeness, occurs everyday, sometimes with disastrous consequences. I admit to being fearful of encountering this situation, so I avoid driving at night, and limit the distance.

Perhaps I am just old-fashioned, and prefer a world with a slower pace, less risk, and less noise. I still believe, however, that it is possible for people to relate to each other in a respectful, positive way that includes the use of good manners. This behavior isn't limited to children or to their parents. I send contributions fairly often in memory of deceased relatives of people who are friends or acquaintances. I receive acknowledgements from churches, synagogues, and organizations, but not always from relatives of the deceased. I remember spending time writing thank-you notes to people who made contributions in memory of the loss of my parents and my husband. When did this practice cease to be necessary? It is a simple courtesy that lets you know that your gesture was appreciated. What is most distressing to me is the way in which people talk to each other. It seems that, instead of teaching the younger generations that the use of good manners has not gone out of style and, in fact, would add to our quality of life, my generation has allowed the lower standards of behavior in today's world to be the acceptable norm. How can this be changed?

An article by Sarah Mahony in *Parents Magazine* discussed the "Brat Pack", children who consistently exhibit rude and obnoxious behavior. The experts that she consulted believe that today's parents are too tired and stressed to discipline their children. Some say also that parents use information on children to analyze and make excuses for their behavior. The examples set by the media with television shows that feature sarcastic put-downs and wisecracks teach children that it's "cool" to act like a brat. Another (and more important) factor is the poor example set by the parents, who exhibit a "give it to me right now" attitude. These experts warn parents that children who are not taught to have good manners will suffer the consequences in later years.

As a mother and grandmother, I am concerned about this problem. I agree with the opinion of the experts on this issue, but I firmly believe that my generation can contribute to the solution. First, we must learn to change our attitude and our behavior. It may be an uphill battle, but we can make a difference. One of the classes that I am privileged to attend, teaches that adherence to basic values of Judaism will help individuals to embrace their spiritual selves and thus achieve a closer connection to God. We learn that we can do this on a daily basis by practicing a positive attitude, trying to find the good in others, and performing "mitzvahs" (good deeds). Not so many years ago I (like today's teenagers) would have rolled my eyes and said, "Yeah, right!" to such an idea. Now, I have begun to practice some of this philosophy, and find that it actually works—at least, some of the time. The message to be learned is that we can't change others, but we can change ourselves. Practicing good manners and random acts of kindness does make a difference. I admit that there are "bumps in the road". I have bad days when I forget this philosophy, and revert to "doing onto others before they can do onto me". I won't give up, though, because the reward is in making a difference by example for my children, grandchildren, and others. Maybe one day I will even feel able to venture into the outside world to dine in a restaurant or watch a movie.

This chapter is included in my book as a message to our generation to set an example for future generations. Good manners should always be a priority with family, friends, and anyone that we encounter socially. We can help make our world a better place, which should help us answer the question "Are the golden years tarnished?"

Chapter Nine

"LIVING ASSERTIVELY"

Are you afraid to tell your hairdresser that you want a different hairstyle? Do you clean your house before the maid arrives? Are you constantly apologizing to relatives and friends for not agreeing to baby-sit, run errands, or otherwise assume responsibilities that don't fit into your busy schedule? If so, you need to read this chapter. It may provide information on how to deal with these issues in a way that allows you to set personal boundaries, and to preserve your relationship with others.

I have practiced living assertively most of my adult life. This behavior is contrary to what was expected of women in my generation. The explanation for this attitude can be found in part in the chapter on relationships. Being a widow for over 20 years probably contributed also. I was always careful to be politically correct in my actions professionally, where there was a price to pay, but in other areas, I took a different course altogether. A few examples come to mind.

My husband and I had sold our property and business the year in which he was diagnosed with terminal cancer. The terms of the sale required our buyer to send a check for a certain amount of money each month for a designated number of years. Most of the time, the check arrived when due. When it didn't, I would make a phone call to the buyer, which usually resulted in the check being mailed. Towards the end of the agreement, I had more difficulty collecting the money. I was hesitant to confront the buyer, so I asked my attorney to send a letter. The money was sent, but I received an angry phone call at work because I had dared to involve an attorney. This was a scary experience but I knew that it was necessary for me to exercise my legal rights. I was relieved when this property agreement ended.

My daughters shared an apartment after graduating from college. One day, the younger daughter called me, very distraught because her apartment (along with others in the complex) was without air conditioning. This occurred during a typical Houston summer, when temperatures were generally in the 90's, with high humidity. I asked if the management had been notified. She assured me that they had been informed, but were given vague messages about when the problem would be resolved. After talking to my daughter, I called the management office. I received the same vague response that she had received. Then "aggressive mom" kicked in. I told the manager that it was intolerable to expect tenants to endure Houston's heat and humidity without air conditioning. I felt certain that the owner could remedy the problem. If not, I was prepared to call Marvin Zindler of channel 13 "Eyewitness News" to see if he could bring about a faster resolution. I then ended the conversation quickly, wondering why I had threatened to call Marvin Zindler, who probably wouldn't have had time for this problem. The next day, my daughters reported that the air conditioning was working. I will never know whether my phone call made the difference, but I don't regret making it.

Several times over the last twenty years, I have changed doctors. Sometimes this was due to being kept waiting for appointments longer than one hour (my limit), sometimes because of the doctor's attitude ("Don't ask questions from information that you received from the Internet. I am the doctor. I will make the diagnosis and prescribe the remedy"). I am currently trying to decide whether to change utility companies because of an excessively high bill resulting from deregulation. I could give other examples, but you get the idea. Sometimes you have to fight back.

Relationship issues can be tricky. Most people are more tolerant of negative behavior from spouses, children, parents, siblings, and friends than from others that we encounter. Even with relatives, it is necessary to set boundaries. The bottom line emphasizes a personal philosophy—you have to take care of yourself first. This isn't being selfish. It is good, common sense. If you are a parent, you know that children learn at a very early age to "push your buttons". This is true of toddlers, teenagers, and adult children. Learn to say "No"—to young children who use tantrums to get what they want, to teenagers who accuse you of being the only parents to enforce a curfew, to adult children who expect free babysitting a little too often. If you are a member of the sandwich generation, trying to balance responsibility for your family, a career, and meeting the needs of aging parents, you might have to tell Mom and Dad that a sister or brother will have to do some of the chauffeuring, shopping, etc., or that a professional service might have to be used from time to time. Husbands and wives, whose relationship should be a priority, also sometimes have to communicate feelings. The husband may not want to attend every family reunion or shop at the mall on Saturdays. The wife may get bored with sports on weekends. Talking about these differences is better for the relationship, and will definitely benefit your physical, mental, and emotional health.

An article in *AARP* Magazine, "Fighting Back", by Ron Barley, advises readers on consumer issues. He uses creative methods in dealing with businesses that take advantage of clients. His tool kit includes simple tips. 1. Know when to fight (when it is worth the time and money involved). 2. Think like a business (Concentrate on how your solution can be a wise business decision.) 3. Channel Dirty Harry. Make like Clint Eastwood. 4. Don't fear Goliath. Find creative ways to win with large corporations. 5. Make nice with the little guy. The person answering the phone can make a difference. 6. Keep it clean. Watch your language and attitude. 7. Protect yourself. Do your homework before dealing with companies. Unfortunately, in today's world, consumers are in need of extra support and assistance just attempting to obtain services or products.

For those readers who are still skeptical of taking an assertive stand, perhaps you could begin by taking small steps. Show your hair stylist several photos that you like, and see if the two of you can agree on the one that would be the most attractive for you. Explain to your friend that you are unable to host a tupperware party because you are having the house painted. Tell your adult children (and other family members) that you want them to have the pleasure of organizing Thanksgiving dinner, and that you will be happy to bring a cranberry casserole. If these suggestions work, you can then graduate to the next level—confronting someone talking too loudly on a cell phone in public or asking parents to keep their kids quiet in a public restaurant.

Being subjected to unacceptable behavior from others could bring some tarnish to our golden years, but if we can learn to deal with this behavior in a creative way, we can then say positively that this will brighten the years for us.

Chapter Ten

"TILL DEATH DO US PART"

In conversations with friends and neighbors (mostly women), I often told them how fortunate they were to still have a husband with whom to enjoy their retirement years. My husband died when our daughters were in college, so we missed the opportunity to spend our golden years together. They quickly agreed, but when the topic discussed was retirement, many of them actually shuddered at the idea. I know that they loved their husbands, but it seemed that the reality of spending all day together frightened them. I decided that this would be an interesting topic to pursue for my book. This chapter explores the issue that faces retired seniors, and includes advice from experts on how to cope.

Ohio State University Extension has an article entitled "Marriage After Retirement". It gives three factors that affect marital quality—timing of retirement, retirement goals, and dealing with household chores. Readers are given four suggestions. 1) Communicate openly, 2) Set boundaries, 3) Prepare for the loss of work, and 4) Designate household tasks. Some of this advice is given in other articles as well.

Marriage Missions International discusses five passages in marriage, each of which requires the couple to complete specified tasks. The article, "Passages of Marriage: Five Growth Stages", advises readers that a strong, healthy ongoing relationship throughout the years is dependent on completing those tasks. In the first passage, young love (first two years), the task is to mold two different persons into one unit. The second passage is realistic love, and covers the third through tenth years of marriage. In this passage, the honeymoon is over, and couples must deal with the realities of everyday life while keeping the marriage intact. In the third passage, comfortable love, years eleven through twenty, couples are challenged with three tasks. They must maintain an individual identity along with their marriage identity, say final good-byes to what may never be accomplished, and overcome the now-or-never syndrome. This is a critical time for marriage break-ups. Having successfully survived the first three passages, the fourth passage, reviving love, years twenty-six through thirty-three, is a final step towards the ultimate goal of a solid marriage. The primary task is to achieve the intimacy of companionship and unity. The fifth passage, year thirty-six and on, brings the final reward for completing the tasks of passages one through four. There are many tasks left. They include: preparation for retirement; celebration of new opportunities; being mentally prepared for shocks and bumps; giving each person his own space; re-apportioning time as his, hers, and ours; scheduling activities according to needs; looking closely at goals; making relationships more meaningful. Transcendent love is a profound and peaceful perspective towards your partner and towards life.

"Love and Marriage in Retirement" gives seven tips for couples to nurture and preserve their relationship in the retirement years. 1) Take the time to get to know each other again. 2) Never while away your hours. 3) Respect the need for privacy and aloneness for yourself and your spouse. 4) Build a social network of family and friends. 5) Be spontaneous with much of your day. 6) Never take the health of yourself or your spouse for granted. 7) Manage your finances together.

The topic of this chapter may seem like a minor problem compared to others facing seniors, but it is still part of the total picture in meeting the challenges of retirement. For couples with no major health or financial problems, it assumes more importance. In today's world, it is almost somewhat of a miracle for marriages to endure for 50 or 60 years. Those that do are based on long-term commitment and hard work. Do whatever works. One friend confided that she and her husband sleep in separate rooms. For them, this was a solution to problems that were affecting the relationship. And remember that there is no law that says that husband and wife have to spend all of their time together. Don't be afraid to explore separate interests. This could add to the quality of the relationship.

Are our golden years tarnished? Looking at this chapter, the question can be answered either way, depending on the status of your marriage. Since many long-term marriages manage to survive, I would conclude that the golden years for many of us are indeed still golden.

Chapter Eleven

"LOVE AND SEX FOR WIDOWS AND WIDOWERS"

Why this topic? Just as there are many ways of grieving after the loss of a spouse, the desire to enter into a new relationship varies with the individual.

In general, men seem to want and need a new relationship more than their female counterparts. If they are basically healthy and financially stable, they want the love and stability of marriage. They want to know deep in their soul that there is someone "there" for them. Fortunately for these men, there is an abundance of women, widowed and/or divorced, who actively pursue relationships. I was amazed at the stories my aunt told me about friends who routinely scanned the obituaries, searching for the names of widowers. They then launched a plan that included invitations to lunch and/or dinner. They had no problem making the first move, and the men often responded. This seems to be a win-win situation.

What about widows? The latest statistics report that widows are more resistant to forming a new relationship, even if it includes marriage. When interviewed, many of them felt that they no longer wanted the role of caretaker, choosing instead to focus on their own lives. This attitude is contrary to what most people believe. For me, it was gratifying to know that many widows shared my feelings. Since I was only 51 when my husband died, I needed time and energy to focus on taking care of myself financially. Within 10 years, I managed to acquire a counseling certification and an LPC, and was financially able to retire shortly before my 60th birthday. By this time, I valued my independence and my privacy, and wasn't interested in pursuing a relationship that could involve limits to both of these luxuries. Instead, I used my newly acquired free time to engage in other activities. I was never bored. During this time, I discovered writing, which has added so much to my life. Do I regret not having a man in my life? After more than 20 years, I still miss my husband, and have no regrets about seeking another relationship.

For widows and widowers who do want and need another relationship, there is advice from the experts.

One Web site stated basic issues to be explored before a decision was made.

First, they advise addressing the question of how long to wait. This, of course, is dependent on circumstances and the grieving process for each individual. Most wait for at least a year, but that might not apply to everyone. A more important consideration is the feelings of children involved.

This leads to the second issue—introducing your prospective spouse to your children, and the children to each other. Give them time to adjust to the idea, and to the new persons involved. If, after meeting and spending time together, one or more children objects to the marriage (or relationship), it is important to remember that the final decision must be made by the couple.

Financial issues are crucial, especially for second marriages. Couples are advised to have a plan for spending money, and whether or not to have separate accounts or a joint account. It is also a good idea to draft new wills, especially with children involved, and to consult with an attorney about a prenuptial agreement. Taking these steps can prevent future problems.

Despite myths to the contrary, research shows that the majority of physically and mentally healthy persons remain sexually active up to age eighty and even beyond. Therefore, couples should be open and honest with each other about sexual needs and preferences. Sexual compatibility can enhance or harm a relationship.

It is important to discuss living arrangements. Will you live in his house, her house, or sell both and buy a new one? What about furniture? What about decorating preferences? Do you need a guest room for family visits? All of these questions should be resolved before the commitment to marriage.

Do either of you have family or financial obligations? No one would want to be surprised after a marriage to learn that his or her in-laws would be living with them or that their new spouse has financial obligations to relatives. In fact, if no agreement can be reached on these issues, the couple might decide that marriage isn't the best idea for them. It is better to know ahead of time than to deal with the possibility of divorce.

Grown children will always be part of the total picture, especially if some of them do not approve of the marriage. Couples have to decide on the amount of contact they will have with their children—how often, what occasions, how long for visits, etc. Even if these issues are resolved, couples are advised not to bring their children into marital conflicts.

Managing family traditions and holidays is another issue that should be discussed. The best solution would be to compromise. Thanksgiving, Christmas, Hanukkah, Passover, and other major holidays can either include both families or alternate between the two. Sometimes, the newlyweds may need to celebrate on their own. That is O.K. too, as long as they offer explanations to family members. As always, the important consideration in every marriage is the needs and desires of the couple.

I don't know whether I have convinced my readers to marry again or not. That wasn't my intention. This chapter was intended to let you know that this is an individual decision, and to give resources for those who do remarry on maximizing a positive relationship. The bottom line is for each person to decide whether remarriage would contribute to a fuller, richer life in their golden years. Either way, through careful planning, the question "Are our golden years tarnished?" can give us the answer we need.

Chapter Twelve

"EXPLORING THE BIG ISSUES"

One of the benefits of retirement is having the time to explore answers to philosophical questions, such as "Who am I?" "Why am I here?" "Will there be an eventual reward for following the rules?" A strong motivation for answering some of these questions is the realization that we don't live forever, and that time is growing short.

One way I have attempted to answer some of these questions is by taking selected courses in Judaism. I am seeking a closer relationship with God, and a reason to believe in the afterlife. The courses are challenging, the class discussions stimulating, but the result not exactly what I had anticipated. After about five years of courses, I remain committed to Conservative Judaism and opposed to extreme views on both the right and the left. I can justify a belief in God, but belief in the existence of an afterlife still eludes me. I am waiting for that "bolt of lightning" to convince me that my soul will continue to exist in some form, with an ultimate reward for good behavior on earth. Maybe that is why I set deadlines to meet goals now. I may never achieve the closer relationship with God. Overcoming the obstacles of observing over 600 commandments is very discouraging. Also, my human nature keeps getting in the way of realizing my spiritual potential. I find it difficult to celebrate the happiness of others when I am having a "bad day". I nurse grudges, and sometimes I want to get even. I also have trouble accepting the idea that the "wrong" people are often rewarded for very unreligious-like behavior. Examples are everywhere—politicians, Hollywood stars, and sports heroes. Why do these people often not only escape punishment for misdeeds, but also continue to enjoy fame and fortune? Waiting for a final reckoning is too long a wait for me. I want them to get their "just desserts" now!

Reading the daily obituaries has become a necessity. I need to know if a family member, friend, or even an acquaintance has died. I look at the age and try to mentally calculate when it will be my turn. This may sound morbid, but it is very practical. Everyone needs a plan for death (whatever your religious affiliation), Not long after our marriage, my husband, with much enthusiasm, informed me that he had purchased a cemetery plot for us in a prime location, including a tree for shade. My response was: He cares enough about me to take care of this; he really believes that our marriage will endure until "death do us part"; and, who cares where the plot is located? We won't know the difference. Today I am grateful that neither of my children will have to deal with this problem. In fact, not too long before his death, my husband and I took care of the details with the funeral home for the service, casket, etc., so that our daughters wouldn't have this burden. I recently attended the funeral of a friend who planned the entire service, including a special ceremony by a professional organization of which she was a member. As I drove home from the service, I thought about putting the finishing touches on my own good-bye, even writing the obituary, but two issues prevent me from doing this. First of all, I am superstitious enough to believe that making final preparations will somehow precipitate my final demise. Also, as stated before, if I am not certain that my soul will "stay around for awhile", or be watching from somewhere, what is the point? I won't know the difference. The only specification I will make is that, if a photo is included with my obituary, it is more recent than high school.

Hopefully, I can make progress towards becoming a better person. A new book by Rabbi Harold Kushner entitled *How Good Do We Have to Be?* discusses perfection as it pertains to our relationship with God. According to Rabbi Kushner, we weren't meant to be perfect, and God loves us even if we aren't. This gives me hope that my imperfect self can gain entry to the next spiritual level (whatever that may be) when my time comes. In the meantime, I will continue to take classes, pray, and do mitzvahs. It can't hurt to cover all of the bases.

My readers will have to decide for themselves how to answer our question after reading this chapter. It is difficult to confront these issues, but I tried to put a positive spin on the topic. The bottom line is that there is much that we do not understand. What we can do is ask questions, seek the answers, and maintain faith.

Chapter Thirteen

"PRESERVING MEMORIES"

One of my columns in "Creative Parenting" was entitled "Preserving Memories". I felt that this was an important responsibility for parents, and wanted to share my thoughts with readers. Photos were especially important in our family, as my husband was a professional photographer. Over the years, when he needed to finish a roll of film for processing, he would use our daughters as willing subjects. Thus, we had numerous photos of them at various stages of their lives. He also took movies (this was before video cameras) of special events. As an anniversary gift one year for my daughters, I decided to have the movies transferred onto a video. When I searched for those precious slices of family history, I discovered, in a shoebox, 36 movies dated and labeled by event. The resulting video (put to music, as we had no sound), is a priceless treasure. It captures not only those wonderful childhood years of my daughters, but the inclusion of other relatives as well, many of whom are deceased. While watching this video, I realized that this gift would become an heirloom for future generations of our family, enabling them to become acquainted, in some small way, with their ancestors.

The production of a family history, complete with family tree, photos, and stories has now become a personal priority. Besides knowledge and appreciation of past generations, what are the benefits of researching family history?

One of the chapters in my first book was "You Can't Escape Your Roots". In this chapter, I explained how having this information could make a difference in the lives of present and future generations. First of all, having medical information is essential. This could result in testing before marriage for possible hereditary diseases, as well as possible treatments. Knowledge of family history can also provide an understanding of who we are—genetically, physically, mentally, and emotionally. I truly believe that this knowledge can help to give us the tools for leading more productive lives.

"Annie's Heart to Heart" is a Web site that adds more benefits. She divides them into three categories. Benefits for children include providing them with a glimpse inside the not-too-distant past, giving them historical accuracy, and sharing memories that are a tangible way to understanding who you are. There are personal benefits. The most important of these are that reflection on the past allows you to realize how much you have achieved, and that you have accomplished many of your dreams and goals. Family benefits include all of the above, but they also leave a priceless legacy for future generations. The life stories of past generations are living testimony to how much your family has dealt with adversity over the years.

Having established the benefits of preserving memories, we need to explore the many hands-on techniques available. There was an article in the Houston Chronicle a few years ago, "Thanks for the Memories", that told you everything you wanted to know about the use of scrapbooks to preserve memories. Since my only experience with scrapbooks was the old-fashioned kind with cut and paste items on a page, I read this article with hope that I could improve my ability in this area. I was rewarded with many ideas for creating scrapbooks, and referral to Web sites for further assistance. The article also gave a history of scrap booking, and a reason for the revival of interest. Today's generation really does want to preserve memories for their children and grandchildren, but they need help. There are groups, such as Creative Memories, that provide this help. In Houston, women meet informally and share ideas for special pages that can include the use of sewing, holiday themes, special background pages, and the incorporation of a theme constructing the scrapbook. Since this article was written, technology has given us other ways to help this creative process.

At Kaboose.com an article on "How to Capture Family Memories Tips on Scrap booking" gives more ideas for keeping the scrapbook. They advise that every photo should be dated, identified, and captioned. News articles should likewise be captioned, with photography added in case the newsprint deteriorates. The use of digital cameras and cell phones to take photos adds another challenge. Users will need to select and print digital photos on a regular basis so that they can be preserved.

The Pickle forum is a blog that provides information on the use of modern technology for the preservation of photos and documents. Video transfer services convert old films into a digital format. Fragile documents of the past can be scanned and preserved digitally. Photos taken with older cameras can be converted to a digital format. For those photos that haven't survived the years in the best condition, there are techniques available for restoration and retouching.

Is all of this time and work worth the effort? Once again, I can call on my personal experience to say that it is. When I worked with my husband in our photo studio, we had many clients who brought in damaged photos to be restored. Some hoped that we had kept the negatives from past occasions to retrieve lost photos. These sad stories usually described a fire or a flood. The loss of these photos was secondary only to the loss of life in these catastrophes. People cared then, and they care now about preserving photos and memories of the past. Without modern techniques, we weren't able to help everyone with this problem. Today's technology allows us to do a better job, so I am grateful that these techniques are available.

Another task for our generation is to preserve the photos and memories of our grandchildren and great grandchildren. Our children, despite all of the technological devices to help them, might not take the time from their busy lives to do this. What a wonderful gift to them to leave behind photo albums and scrapbooks to keep and be able to share with their children when they are old enough to appreciate their value.

This is one of my favorite chapters. I wish that everyone could appreciate the value of preserving family memories for future generations. I don't even need to ask the question, do I? If you have read this chapter, and it has given you an awareness of this responsibility, you can definitely count this as a positive in your golden years.

Chapter Fourteen

"GRAND PARENTING AND GREAT GRAND PARENTING"

In my "Creative Parenting" column I devoted two articles to grandparents raising grandchildren. I have friends who have assumed the responsibility of raising their grandchildren. When I observed the impact of this experience (both positive and negative) on their lives, I decided to research the topic. The results of this research were surprising.

Studies reported that in the year 2000, approximately four million children (about 6% of the population) lived with their grandparents compared with 4% in 1980. An October, 2001 fact sheet by AARP reported that more than six million children are living in households headed by grand-parents. Some of the reasons for this trend are: 1) increasing numbers of single parent families, 2) the high rate of divorce, 3) teenage pregnancies, 4) AIDS, 5) incarceration of parents, 6) substance abuse by parents, 7) death or disability of parents, 8) parental abuse and neglect. How many of you would be prepared to accept this responsibility at a time in your life when you could finally be free to concentrate on taking care of yourself? That is a difficult question to answer, and depends on the physical, mental, emotional, and financial condition of the individual.

There are basically three types of grandparent caregivers. Custodial grandparents have legal custody of their grandchildren. They provide daily care and make decisions related to school, activities, etc. The second type of grandparent caregivers is the "living with" grandparents. These grandparents provide daily care for their grandchildren, but do not have legal custody. The parents may or may not live in the home. Day care grandparents are the third type of caregivers. Their focus is on helping the child's parent and on fulfilling their own needs. They are less affected by the care-giving role.

All grandparents involved in raising their grandchildren face special challenges. Legally, unless they seek full custody and/or guardianship, they are not entitled to financial compensation or medical benefits. They also have to balance responsibility for their grandchildren's well being with the quality of the relationship with the parents, who may want this arrangement to be temporary. They must also cope with physical, mental, and emotional demands of being the main caregivers for children at a time when they normally look forward to retirement and a less stressful routine.

I conducted interviews with friends who had assumed the responsibility of raising their grandchildren. In spite of the challenges and hardships, each one found this a rewarding experience. The reward was in watching their grandchildren grow into healthy, responsible men and women under their guidance.

One Web site offered tips for raising grandchildren. Set up a daily routine. Make your home a welcoming place that is child friendly. Work on communication skills. Practice positive discipline. Set up rules. Read to your grandchildren. Get computer savvy. Join a support group. Take up an outdoor activity. Take care of yourself. Take parenting classes. Learn to say "No".

Many Web sites gave resources for grandparents. These references are at the end of the book.

As I close out this chapter, I once again ask the question, "Are our golden years tarnished"? For those of you who have the responsibility and the privilege of raising grandchildren, the answer will probably be "No". Either way, this experience will become a greater part of our future in the golden years.

Chapter Fifteen

"REFLECTION"

In my first book, I included a chapter like this one. In that chapter, I challenged my readers to ask themselves if they regretted the choices they had made in their lives. Most of us, I believe, make decisions based on the information that we have at that time. If these decisions ultimately have a negative impact on our lives or on others, then it is our responsibility to make the necessary changes. I also asked if anyone would trade places with someone else if it were possible to do so. To my surprise, I discovered that most of us (myself included) would not opt to trade. As we have experienced over the years, no one has a "perfect" life. Finally, I asked my readers if they had discovered a special purpose in their lives, and in what way they were committed to fulfilling that purpose.

This book has taken a different approach, so the reflection will also be different. I hope that my readers will have a clearer understanding of the challenges facing them as seniors in the 21st century. I also hope that they are aware of the many resources available to seniors. Most of all, I hope that all seniors will accept their role as a powerful source of influence and guidance on future generations. Whether the issue is diversity, the environment, or the preservation of basic values, we need to find a way to communicate our message to the younger generation.

Of course, I have to end the book as I began it, by asking the question, "Are our golden years tarnished?" I hope, for most of you, the answer will be "No."

Bibliography

Books, pamphlets, articles

Centers for Medicare & medical Services. <u>Medicare & You 2010.</u> government document.

Clements, Donna. B.A. <u>Manager, social Security Information Services. Guide to Social Security</u>: Louisville, Kentucky. Mercer, 2010.

Kushner, Harold S. <u>When Bad Things Happen to Good People.</u> New York: Avon Books, 1981.

Manning, Diane. <u>Life is too complicated . . . When do we start having fun?</u> Houston, Texas. Kinglsley Literary Services, 2007.

Neeld, Elizabeth Harper, PhD. <u>Seven Choices</u> New York: Crown Publishers, 1990.

Tatelbaum, Judy, MSW. "<u>Surviving the Holidays When Someone You Love Has Died.</u>" Bereavement Magazine.

Viorst, Judith. <u>Necessary Losses.</u> New York: Simon & Schuster, 1998.

Web Sites

AARP Grief and Loss Programs." AARP

"Activities for Seniors." Love to Know.

"Activity Ideas for Retired Seniors." Love to Know.

"Aging and Vision Changes." Perkins Scout.

"Aging can increase vulnerability to problems." Centre for Addiction and Mental Health.

"Americans Living Longer, Healthier Lives due to Medical Innovation and New Therapies." Earth Times.

"Annie's Heart to Heart." history from the heart.com.

Association of Personal Historians. Personal historians.org.

"Awesome Anti-Aging Brain Games." Masters of Healthcare.

Blogs—The Pickle Forum. Pickleforum.ning.com.

"Books for seniors." Amazon.com.

"Brain Fitness 101." Marbles the Brain Store.

"Coping with Grief." Caregivers Library.org.

"Coping with Grief and Loss." About.com.

"Coping with the Loss of a Loved One." Lifestyle.

"Coping with the Loss of a Spouse." About.com.

"Creating Memories—Scrap booking Supplies & ideas. Photo Albums & Scrapbooks." Creative memories.com.

"Dealing with Death: Letting Go of the Ones We Love." Health & Wellness.

"Degree Programs—Find Top Online Schools." College Degree Network.

"Education Can Be a Lifelong Process." Education Guide.

"Education for Senior Citizens." Senior resource.com.

"Educational Opportunities for Senior Citizens." Seniors—site.com.

"Family History, Family Tree, and Genealogy." familysearch.org.

Fergus, Mary Ann. "Thanks for the Memories." Houston Chronicle 2003.

"Find Your Degree from Leading Online Colleges." Degree Search Network.

"Five Types of Games that Keep Your Mind Fit." *www.sixwise.com.*

"For Widows and widowers Who Are Considering Remarriage."
Marriage Missions International.

"Games and Activities for Senior Citizens." Love to Know.

"Genealogy Search Family Trees & Vital Records." Archives.com.

"Giving Up Driving: Easing the Transition." Caring.com.

Grandparents Raising Grandchildren. "Becoming Parents Again for our Children's Children." grand-parenting. Suite 101.com.

Grandparents Raising Grandchildren. "Facts for Families." Adolescent Psychiatry.

"Grandparents Raising Grandchildren." Grandparents as Parents. About.com.

"Grandparents Raising Grandchildren." Child Welfare Information Gateway.

"Grandparents Raising Grandchildren. "Parenting Help for Second Generation Parents." Inter-child relationships. Suite 101.com.

"Grandparents Raising Grandchildren, Part One." Manning, Diane. Life is too Complicated. Houston, Texas. Kingsbury Literary Services, 2007.

"Grandparents Raising Grandchildren Part Two." Manning, Diane. Life is too Complicated. Houston, Texas. Kingsbury Literary Services, 2007.

"Grandparents Raising Grandchildren." USA.gov.

Grandparent Rights. "Do Grandparents Have the Rights They Should?" Grandparents.com.

"Healthy Aging Tips: How to Feel Young and Live Life to the Fullest." Help guide.org.

"Help, Lord!" I'm Having a Senior Moment." Amazon.com.

"How to Capture Family Memories: Tips on Scrap-booking." Kaboose.com.

"How to Cross Train Your Brain," Articlesbase.

"How to Cope After the Death of Your spouse." About.com.

"How to Get Free Education as a Senior Citizen." eHow.com.

"How to Live a Longer and Healthier Life." eHow.com.

"Hurting Holidays Coping Tips for Your first Holiday Alone." About.com.

"Improving Your Memory: tips and Techniques to Improve Memory." Help guide.org.

Jewish Gen.org.

Jobs for Senior Citizens: Working After Retirement." Senior-finances. Suite101.com.

"Learning Well Combating the Changes of Aging." LearningWell.org.

"Love and Marriage in Retirement." Selfgrowth.com.

"Marriage After the Death of Your Spouse." eHow.com.

"Marriage After Retirement." Ohio State University Extension Senior Series.

Memoir Writing & Teaching Resources. Soleil Life story Network. Turning memories.com.

www.MyMedicare.gov.

www.medicare.gov.

"Nana Technology tools help seniors be independent." USA Today.com.

"Passages of Marriage: Five Growth Stages." Marriage Missions International.

"Passion: The Key to a Longer and Healthier Life." Third Age Articles.

"Phased Retirement, Alternative Option for prospective Retirees." AARP.

"Post Retirement Jobs—Jobs for Seniors—Jobs for Retirees—resume and job search tips." Post retirement jobs.com.

"Preserving Memories." Manning, Diane. Life is too Complicated. *Dmanning39@sbcglobal.net.*

"Secrets to a Longer, Healthier and Happier Life." La Dolce Living.

"Senior Activities." Love to Know.

"Senior citizen Groups." Love to Know.

"Senior Citizen Organizations." Love to Know.

"Senior Moments." AuthorsBookshop.com.

"Senior Service." Corporation for National & Community Service.

"Senior Travel." Love to Know.

"The 7 Pillars to Longer Healthier Life." Millionaire Healer.com.

www.SocialSecurity.gov.

"State Fact sheets fir Grandparents and Other Relatives Raising Children." AARP.

"Strategies for coping with hearing loss." Health.

"The Strength of Your beliefs." About.com.

"Tell Your Longevity Success Story—Success Aging Stories." About.com.

"Tips for living a longer and healthier life." letmeget.com.

"Tips on How to Get Through the Holidays if You've Lost a Loved One." Lifestyle.

"When Older Friends and Loved Ones Die." My Option Health.

"Widowers and Remarriage." Users.ren.com.

"With Friends Aplenty, Many Widows Choose Single-hood." The New Old Age Blog.

About the Author

Diane Manning is a native Houstonian. She has one brother, Cantor David Axelrad, who resides in Houston. She credits the values taught by her parents, Max and Leah Axelrad, and her close family ties for her accomplishments.

In 1966, she married Arthur A. Manning, owner of Work of Art photography studio. Their union produced two daughters, Marla Gayle (43), and Lauren Jill (41). She and her husband centered their lives on raising their daughters and operating their photography studio. Her husband died in 1990.

Diane has seventeen years of experience as a teacher and a guidance counselor. She has also served as a consultant for several private schools in Houston, and has given programs on various parenting and senior-related topics. She has a Master of Science in Education, certification as a guidance counselor, and is a Licensed Professional Counselor.

She has been a columnist with a local newspaper for nine years with a column entitled "Creative Parenting". She has published two previous books. *Life is too Complicated-When do we Start Having Fun?* is an informational book written in a humorous style for seniors. *And Baby Makes Three* is based on the first five years of her experience as a Columnist.